AR PTS: 1.0

D0713453

Celebrity Biographies

Robert Pattinson

SHINING STAR

BY MICHAEL A. SCHUMAN

Enslow Publishers, Inc.
40 Industrial Road
Box 398
Berkeley Heights, NJ 07922
USA
http://www.enslow.com

Library of Congress Cataloging-in-Publication Data

Schuman, Michael.

    Robert Pattinson : shining star / by Michael A. Schuman.
        p. cm. — (Hot celebrity biographies)
    Includes index.
    Summary: "Read about Robert Pattinson's life—from a young child to a model to a film star in the Twilight series"—
        Provided by publisher.
    ISBN 978-0-7660-3872-1
    1. Pattinson, Robert, 1986—Juvenile literature. 2. Motion picture actors and actresses—Great Britain—Biography—
        Juvenile literature. I. Title.
    PN2598.P36S35 2011
    792.02'8092—dc22
    [B]
                          2010048013

Paperback ISBN 978-1-59845-284-6

Printed in the United States of America

072012 Lake Book Manufacturing, Inc., Melrose Park, IL

10 9 8 7 6 5 4 3 2

To Our Readers: We have done our best to make sure all Internet Addresses in this book were active and appropriate when we went to press. However, the author and publisher have no control over and assume no liability for the material available on those Internet sites or on other Web sites they may link to. Any comments or suggestions can be sent by e-mail to comments@enslow.com or to the address on the back cover.

♻ Enslow Publishers, Inc., is committed to printing our books on recycled paper. The paper in every book contains 10% to 30% post-consumer waste (PCW). The cover board on the outside of each book contains 100% PCW. Our goal is to do our part to help young people and—the environment—too!

Photo Credits: AP Images/Charles Sykes, pp. 4, 41; AP Images/Chris Pizzello, pp. 12, 37; AP Images/Denis Poroy, p. 7; AP Images/Domenico Stinellis, p. 16; AP Images/Evan Agostini, p. 38; AP Images/Graylock.com, p. 26; AP Images/Joel Ryan, pp. 10, 30; AP Images/Katsumi Kasahara, p. 33; AP Images/Kirsty Wigglesworth, p. 24; AP Images/ Koji Sasahara, pp. 18, 22; AP Images/Matt Sayles, pp. 6, 34, 36, 43; AP Images/Rick Bowmer, p. 32.

Cover Photo: AP Images/Matt Sayles (Robert Pattinson arriving at the *Vanity Fair* Oscar Party on February 22, 2009.)

Contents

Waiting for the Star

At the end of 2007, Robert Pattinson was a little-known British actor. The young man had achieved a bit of fame by appearing in two of the Harry Potter movies. But for the previous four years, he only had been in movies made for British television or shown in few theaters.

But on November 17, 2008, thousands of young people mobbed Hollywood Boulevard in Los Angeles to see Pattinson. The movie version of the book *Twilight* was to be shown for the first time. The setting was the legendary Grauman's Chinese Theater. The theater is famous for its courtyard where footprints of many of Hollywood's stars are imbedded in cement.

Pattinson was following a Hollywood tradition by personally attending the premier of a movie he starred in. When he arrived at the theater, the screams of the thousands of people were deafening. Fans and professional photographers alike called out his name. They begged him to pose for photos. Reporters shoved each other aside

◀ *As a big star, Robert Pattinson got to leave his handprints at the Planet Hollywood restaurant in New York City.*

As his fans cheer in the background, Robert Pattinson arrives at the premiere of the first Twilight movie.

trying to get a quote from Pattinson. Girls wanted more than his autograph. They wanted to touch him and run their fingers through his trademark disheveled hair.

But what had turned Robert into an idol in little more than a year? The tale is a dream story of Hollywood.

"ROBERT WAS COVERED IN JAM"

Robert Pattinson was born in the cozy town of Barnes, England. Barnes is not far from the big city of London Robert's father, Richard, imported classic cars for a living. His mother, Clare, worked as a talent scout for a modeling agency. Robert has two older sisters, Victoria and Elizabeth, known by her nickname, Lizzy.

As a baby, Robert had blond hair and a pudgy build. It was not easy being the little brother. Victoria and Lizzy dressed him in girls' clothes and forced him to play house. They introduced him to their friends as their sister, Claudia.

When not being made to play with his sisters, Robert often played alone, for he was a shy child. He does not remember having a lot of toys. Robert told *Empire* magazine, "I just used to play with a pack of cards all the time. I'd pretend the cards were other things. I liked any toy what didn't involve playing with other children."

Robert's parents were strong believers in the arts. So they arranged for him to take piano lessons when he was about three. When he was roughly five, he started learning classical guitar. But he had his share of fun outside music, too. His aunt, Diana Nutley, remembered a party in the garden of her home. She told *Life & Style* magazine, "We had a wonderful game to see how many doughnuts we could eat without licking our lips. It's impossible—Robert was covered in jam."

To Private School

Robert's parents paid to send him to a private school when he was four. It was an all-male school called Tower House Boys Preparatory School in west London. The school's secretary, Caroline Booth, remembered that Robert was only a fair student, but truly enthusiastic about one subject. She told writer Flora Stubbs, "He wasn't a particularly academic child but he always loved drama."

Young Robert acted in his first school play at age six. His role was the King of Hearts in a play that one of his teachers wrote. It was titled *Spell for a Rhyme*.

In addition to acting talent, Robert became known in school for a less likeable trait—sloppiness. A school newsletter article in 1998 stated that twelve-year-old Robert was "a runaway winner of last term's Form Three untidy desk award." (A "form" is the same as a grade level in the United States.)

His acting and messy desk aside, Robert was an average Joe among his fellow students. He told *the London Sunday*

ROBERT THE SCHOOLBOY

Pattinson confided to the BBC, "I was a bit of a loner at school, quite antisocial. My first kiss was when I was twelve, but I didn't have a girlfriend until I was eighteen." Some of his former classmates disagree and say Pattinson was more popular than he now admits.

Still, he could not always escape being bullied. One day at school someone took the shoelaces off his shoes. Pattinson went the rest of the day wearing his shoes without shoelaces. As if to prove he wouldn't let the bully get the better of him, he decided to keep wearing his shoes without laces. That became a kind of Pattinson trademark in school.

Times, "I wasn't with the cool gang, or the uncool ones. I was transitional, in between . . . I wasn't involved in much at school and I was never picked for any of the teams." Outside of school, Robert liked watching television, especially cartoons. When he was about ten he took his first job, a paper route.

GOODBYE TO "CLAUDIA"

At twelve, Robert had to adapt to changes in his life. He left Tower House Boys Preparatory School and entered Harrodian School. Like Tower House, Harrodian is a private school near London. Unlike Tower House, students of both genders attend Harrodian. In addition, Harrodian has extra facilities. These include a heated outdoor swimming pool, a music center, and drama studios.

▲ Pattinson's sister, Lizzy, grew up to be a singer who had three Top 20 hits on the United Kingdom charts. She also sang on the Milk & Sugar song "Let the Sun Shine."

Being in a school for both genders made Robert feel more comfortable around girls. That included his sisters. He finally stood up to Victoria and Lizzy, He told them he no longer wanted to be Claudia. That stage of his life was finally over.

While he continued to deliver newspapers, he took another job. Because his mother worked in modeling, she knew a lot of people in the business. So, soon Robert was getting some modeling work.

In the classroom, Pattinson continued to enjoy the arts. He used his musical talents to front a rap trio when he was fourteen. Rap has its roots in American inner cities. Most rap songs are about young people growing up amid crime and poverty. Pattinson said to writer Sona Charaipotra of *The New York Times* that his trio was "pretty hard-core for three private school kids from suburban London." But he added that his mother often ruined the boys' attempt at being hard core. He told Charaipotra that often in the middle of their practice sessions, "[m]y mum's like, cramping our style, popping her head in to ask, 'You boys want a sandwich?'"

From Rapper to Actor

Robert was still modeling and singing in his rap trio in his early teens. But he told the BBC that one day while in a restaurant, everything changed.

He was having dinner with his father, who made polite conversation with some girls at a nearby table. He asked where they had been. They answered that they had been at a local acting school called the Barnes Theater Company.

Robert's father urged him to try out for classes there. Perhaps he knew that Rob's heart was not in his studies. Or perhaps he recalled Rob enjoying acting as a child at Tower House. Rob told the BBC simply, "I don't know what his intentions were, but I went."

However, Pattinson later told a reporter from *You* magazine that he joined Barnes because a girl he liked was part of the theater company. Whatever the reason, Robert was about to begin to get a real education in acting.

◀ *Robert Pattinson sits in the Four Seasons hotel in Beverly Hills, California. Before he hit it big, Robert took a number of small roles in plays and movies that were only shown on TV.*

FAREWELL TO MODELING

About this time, his modeling career started to fade. Pattinson told *Closer* magazine that as he grew he lacked the look the modeling agencies wanted. By the time he was sixteen, he had stopped modeling. He was spending more and more time at the Barnes Theater Company. He admitted he liked the theater, and he also thought acting would be a good way to meet girls.

Every theater company needs talented people to work backstage. Backstage workers do everything from paint scenery to handle stage lights. Barnes Theater Company was no different. At first, Robert worked behind the scenes.

Soon, however, he auditioned for a part in the Barnes production of *Guys and Dolls*, a popular musical play that had originally premiered on Broadway in New York City in 1950. Rob got a small part as a dancer. Then he got a part in another great American play to be performed at Barnes: *Our Town.*

As he had hoped, Rob did meet girls. He dated off and on, but never had a serious girlfriend.

A DEAL WITH HIS FATHER

Since Robert was not doing well in his studies, his father, Richard, threatened to take him out of Harrodian. Robert was determined to show his father he was not a quitter. He insisted that he wanted to graduate. Robert's father made a deal with his son. Robert would have to pay the tuition, or school costs, to keep attending the private school. If Robert earned good grades, his father would pay him back.

Robert's next acting role was in a Barnes Theater Company's production titled *Tess of the D'Urbervilles*. It is based on a classic novel written by Englishman Thomas Hardy in 1891. Robert had a big part, and it turned out to be his first break. A member of one audience was friends with a famous casting agent named Mary Selway.

Selway met Robert. She liked him and believed he had a future in movies. She arranged for Robert to play a small supporting role in a film version of *Vanity Fair*. It is a famous British novel published in 1848 by William Thackeray.

MARY SELWAY

In the movie business, Mary Selway was as well known as many actors. She was born March 14, 1936, in Norwich, England, and enrolled in a school of the dramatic arts at age thirteen. Mary was too shy to appear on stage. But that did not keep her from entering show business. She first worked as a production assistant on British television programs.

She gradually became a casting agent. She went on to cast films for great movie directors including Stephen Spielberg, Sydney Pollack, and Robert Altman. The most famous movie she helped cast was *Raiders of the Lost Ark*. Mary Selway died of cancer on April 21, 2004, at age sixty-eight.

▲ From left, screenplay writer Julian Fellowes, Reese Witherspoon, director Mira Nair, and actor James Purefoy pose for a photo while they promote Vanity Fair at the Venice Film Festival on September 5, 2004. Robert Pattinson played Reese Witherspoon's son in the movie. However, his scenes were cut.

Robert played Rawdy Crawley, the son of a woman named Becky Sharp. Becky, the lead character, was played in the movie by actress Reese Witherspoon. What is interesting is that in real life, Robert is just ten years younger than Witherspoon. Several years later, Witherspoon gave her impression of Pattinson: "I remember he was verrrrry handsome. I was like, `I really have a handsome son!'"

However, Robert suffered a fate that many actors have faced. After a movie is filmed, the director often decides if some scenes don't work. *Vanity Fair*'s director, Mira Nair, did not like the way Pattinson's character interacted with Witherspoon's. All of Pattinson's scenes were cut from the movie before it was shown in theaters. However, they were left in the DVD version of *Vanity Fair*. Plus, he was able to get some valuable experience working on a real film.

Becoming Cedric Diggory

Soon after Pattinson's experience with *Vanity Fair*, he was offered another small role. This movie would be shown not in theaters, but on television in Europe. And this time, his part stayed in the film.

The movie was a fantasy that takes place in northern Europe in the Middle Ages. It is titled *Ring of the Nibelungs*, and it is based on ancient German myths. Author J.R.R. Tolkien used some of the same myths as the basis for his Lord of the Rings books. *Ring of the Nibelungs* had all the elements of a thrilling adventure, with royal romance, cursed treasure, and even the slaying of a dragon.

Robert played Giselher, the younger brother of Princess Kriemhild and King Gunther. It is a small but important role, since Giselher is involved with important plot twists.

Taking the role in *Ring of the Nibelungs* meant a major inconvenience for Rob. The movie was filmed in South

◀ *Pattinson's first hit movie that he acted in was* Harry Potter and the Goblet of Fire.

Africa, nearly 6,000 miles from England. At the time, Robert was still a student at Harrodian. He was as determined as ever to prove to his father he could earn good grades. So he packed his text books and class notes along with his clothing and prepared to travel to South Africa.

A WONDERFUL OFFER

Shortly before he was about to depart, he was contacted by Mary Selway. She heard of a role she thought would be perfect for Robert. It was the part of Cedric Diggory in the movie *Harry Potter and the Goblet of Fire*. Diggory is a handsome and almost too perfect Hogwarts student who is Harry's romantic rival. This was the fourth movie based on author J.K. Rowling's Harry Potter book series. Movie experts expected it would be just as big as the previous Potter films. Appearing in a potential blockbuster could be a fantastic boost for the career of an unknown actor.

Selway arranged for Robert to meet the movie's director, Mike Newell. On the day before he was to leave for South Africa, Pattinson got together with Newell and some of the movie's casting agents. Newell later told the *London Evening Standard*, "Robert Pattinson was born to play the role; he's quintessentially English, with chiseled public-schoolboy good looks."

Pattinson left for South Africa, not yet knowing if he had landed the role of Cedric Diggory. While in South Africa, he put his efforts into making *Ring of the Nibelungs*. During slow times during filming, Robert studied for his final tests. Even though *Ring of the Nibelungs* was still being filmed, Pattinson was given permission to return to England to take the tests at Harrodian. Robert received an A and two Bs in his final three courses. His father paid him back the tuition money. And Robert learned what he could accomplish if he worked hard.

The filming of *Ring of the Nibelungs* lasted about four months. The day he returned home, the staff from the Harry Potter movie called to ask him to do one more audition. It was at the audition that he was told he got the part of Cedric Diggory.

A Tough Choice

Robert had just graduated high school, and had to make a decision. He had proven that he could be a good student. He considered going to college. Yet, a golden opportunity to act in a major movie had arrived.

Acting is a difficult business for those who want a steady income. While some actors are superstars, the majority can go for years without an acting job. A college education could have led Robert to a job in a more secure business.

It was a serious choice for a seventeen-year-old. He finally decided he would take the chance to turn his favorite hobby—acting—into his dream job.

▲ *From the left, Harry Potter and the Goblet of Fire actors Emma Watson, Katie Leung, and Robert Pattinson have some fun with director Mike Newell.*

Before the actual filming of *Harry Potter and the Goblet of Fire* began, Robert was cast to play a part in a different story. This was not a movie, but a stage play. Unlike the work at Barnes Theater Company, this was a professional play to be performed in the respected Royal Court Theater in London. It was titled *The Woman Before*.

FIRED FROM THE CAST

Pattinson never acted in the play. He was fired and replaced by another actor before the play premiered.

STUNT WORK

Since Robert Pattinson was thin and not overly muscular, he was made to work with a personal trainer to bulk up so he could better resemble Cedric. Robert confessed, "It (the training program) was run by one of the stunt team, who are the most absurdly fit guys in the world. I can't even do ten press-ups [push-ups]! I did about three weeks of that and, in the end, I think he got so bored of trying to force me to do it that he wrote it all down so that I could do it at home."

In time, Pattinson got into shape. That was good, because some scenes were tough. In scenes taking place in a maze, Robert was yanked by ropes and often ran into hedges. Since the scenes had to be shot several times, he banged again and again into actor Daniel Radcliffe, who plays Harry.

In some swimming scenes, Robert had to act underwater in a massive tank. He practiced scuba diving before the scenes were shot.

Why was he fired? There are different explanations, but no definite answer. One says that he got sick and missed too many rehearsals. However, Pattinson told *You* magazine he was fired for taking too many risks with his role.

Ring of the Nibelungs was first shown in Germany in November 2004. It was later aired in Great Britain, Australia, and the United States. Unfortunately, the majority of

▼ *The young cast of* Harry Potter and the Goblet of Fire *poses for a photo. Included are, from left: Stanislav Ianevski, Clemence Poesy, Rupert Grint, Emma Watson, Daniel Radcliffe, Katie Leung, and Robert Pattinson.*

critics blasted the movie. Some said it was hard to follow. Others said the script was weak and that the lead actors' performances were poor. Because Pattinson's role was small, his acting reputation was not affected by the dismal reviews.

Soon enough, filming on *Harry Potter and the Goblet of Fire* began in and around London. Filming a Harry Potter movie is not like working on stage or in a standard movie drama. There is a lot of action, and Robert was called on to perform in scenes that required difficult stunts. Cedric is a seventeen-year-old boy in tremendous physical condition.

As if the physical acts were not nerve-wracking enough, Robert got anxious around his costars. Some—such as Ralph Fiennes, who plays Lord Voldemort; Alan Rickman, who plays Severus Snape; Maggie Smith, as Professor McGonagall; and Michael Gambon as Albus Dumbledore—are among Great Britain's best known and talented. Pattinson was not sure if he fit in. He admitted to the BBC, "I was so conscious of the fact that I didn't know what I was doing, I used to sit on the side of the set, throwing up."

Like the other Harry Potter movies, *Harry Potter and the Goblet of Fire* was a huge hit. And Pattinson was suddenly famous. *The London Times* wrote about Pattinson, "This fresh-faced, photogenic 18-year-old so oozes charm and likeability that casting directors are predicting a big future."

A Life of Independents

One would think that having performed in a blockbuster hit, Robert Pattinson would act in similar movies. But Pattinson went on a different career path.

He moved to a London neighborhood called Soho. Soho is the home of serious but often low-paid artists and writers. Many who live there look down upon stars who are mainly interested in fame and glamour.

Pattinson spent most of his days playing guitar. He performed at London clubs in jam sessions. Sometimes he would take to the stage with a local rock band that was thrown together. Perhaps Pattinson's life surrounded by the artists of Soho influenced his decision to turn down more teen hero roles like Cedric Diggory. His next projects were made by independent filmmakers. They worked with a fraction of the money spent on making Harry Potter movies. Pattinson might have been trying to prove that he wanted to be seen as a serious actor and not just a handsome face.

◀ *Robert Pattinson attends the premiere of* Harry Potter and the Order of the Phoenix. *However, his character only had a few scenes in this movie.*

ROBERT PATTINSON IN A HORROR MOVIE?

His next project was a horror mystery titled *The Haunted Airman*. Pattinson played a physically challenged military veteran who keeps having flashbacks to his war experiences. Pattinson's movie after *The Haunted Airman* was a drama about a single, teenage mother. It was called *The Bad Mother's Handbook*. Pattinson played a nerdy boy named Daniel Gale. Daniel is the complete opposite of the handsome and gallant Cedric Diggory. Both movies were shown only on British television. Neither received wonderful reviews. In fact, most of the reviews of *The Bad Mother's Handbook* were horrible.

In 2007, the movie *Harry Potter and the Order of the Phoenix* was released. Like the other Potter movies, it was a grand success. Pattinson played Cedric Diggory once more, but only in flashbacks. He had much less screen time than in *Harry Potter and the Goblet of Fire*. Pattinson was more interested in getting back to artsy films with small budgets.

He appeared in two more independent movies: a short film titled *The Summer House*, and the comedy/drama *How to Be*. Neither was seen by large audiences. However, two things made *How to Be* a noteworthy step in Pattinson's film career. The movie earned Pattinson his first acting award: best actor in a feature from the Strasbourg International Film Festival, in Strasbourg, France. The movie sound track also featured three original songs performed by Pattinson.

The fact that not many people saw either movie did not stop Pattinson from continuing on the same career path. In 2007, he began work on yet another small budget movie. It was a drama about one of the twentieth century's most famous artists: Salvador Dali. The movie was titled *Little Ashes*, after the name of one of Dali's paintings.

After Pattinson finished filming *Little Ashes*—but before it was released—he received another movie offer. It would change his life forever.

The book *Twilight* by Stephenie Meyer was published in 2005. It was an immediate hit, and it continued to be a best-seller for the next few years. In the novel, a human teenage girl named Bella Swan falls in love with a teenage vampire named Edward Cullen. Three sequels followed. After the first book became a hit, it was obvious that some movie studio would produce a filmed version. In July 2007 it was announced that a production company named Summit Entertainment would make a movie of *Twilight*.

SALVADOR DALI

Salvador Dali was born in Figueres, Spain, in 1904. He was known for his long, loopy mustache and his paintings done in a strange style called surrealism. Much of his artwork presents landscapes in dreamlike settings. His most famous paintings feature melting watches representing the persistence of memory. Dali often made outlandish statements, such as, "I started calling myself a genius to impress people, and ended up being one." Dali died in 1989.

Teenage actress Kristen Stewart was cast to play Bella. But who would play Edward? *Twilight*'s most die-hard fans posted their suggested on Meyer's Web site. These included Hayden Christenson, Orlando Bloom, and Jackson Rathbone. Pattinson was one of several actors invited to audition for the role. While Rathbone did not get the role of Edward, he was cast to play Jasper.

Pattinson was not sure he even wanted the part. He had not read the book. When he finally did read it, he asked himself whether he would be able to play the dashing yet mystical Edward Cullen.

KRISTEN STEWART

Kristen Jaymes Stewart was born on April 9, 1990 in Los Angeles. Both her parents worked behind the scenes in the movie business. Despite her parents' jobs, she was first discovered acting in a school Christmas play when she was eight. Her first major role was in the thriller movie, *Panic Room*, when she was twelve. Kristen has appeared in more than two dozen movies. Although she is best known as Bella in *The Twilight Saga* movies, she showed she could take on other roles when she played rock guitarist Joan Jett in *The Runaways* in 2010.

Still, he went to several auditions in front of the movie's director, Catherine Hardwicke. He auditioned on his own, and then with Kristen Stewart. It was important that Stewart and whoever played Edward were believable as a couple. Hardwicke told the Twilight blog, atwilightkiss.com, "I'm just there with the camera and kind of feeling the magic sort of come alive. And that chemistry, it was pretty exciting." By "chemistry," Hardwicke means the natural way both Stewart and Pattinson reacted to each other. Hardwicke decided to offer Pattinson the part.

COULD ROBERT PATTINSON BE EDWARD?

However, the bosses at Summit Entertainment were not sure Pattinson was right for Edward. They did not think he was handsome enough. With his messy hair and slight build, they felt he did not look like Edward. Hardwicke told Lev Grossman of *Time* magazine, "He was disheveled. He was a different weight. His hair was different and dyed black. [He had dyed it for his role as Salvador Dali.] He was all sloppy. The studio head said, `You want to cast this guy as Edward Cullen?' I said yeah. And he said, 'Do you think you can make him look good.' I said yes, I do."

The bosses at Summit were not the only people unsure if Pattinson would make a good Edward. Die-hard fans of *Twilight* were outraged. Most knew him only as Cedric Diggory, a dashing Englishman. Edward is a conflicted American. Could the young man who played Cedric Diggory make Edward Cullen seem real?

In December 2007, Stephenie Meyer responded to critics by posting on her blog: "I am ecstatic with Summit's choice for Edward. There are very few actors who can look both dangerous and beautiful at the same time, and even fewer who I can picture in my head as Edward. Robert Pattinson is going to be amazing."

Still, Pattinson knew it would not be easy to win over *Twilight* fanatics. He had to do much to get ready to film the movie. As with his role as Cedric Diggory, Pattinson met with a personal trainer to get into better shape. Edward Cullen is very strong, and Robert had to look the part. He also had to learn to play baseball. There is a baseball scene in *Twilight* that greatly affects the plot. Being from Great Britain, Pattinson knew nothing about the sport.

◀ During the filming of Twilight, director Catherine Harwicke tells Robert Pattinson how he should act in a scene from the movie.

▶ *Twilight* stars Robert Pattinson, Kristen Stewart, and Taylor Lautner promote the film in Japan.

By the summer of 2008, Hardwicke and her crew were knee-deep in the filming of *Twilight*. So many of the book's fans were looking forward to the movie that newspapers, magazines, blogs, and television programs did features on it months before it was released. Photos of Pattinson and Stewart in character as Edward and Bella were published everywhere. The cable network MTV seemed to be *Twilight*'s best friend. Every Tuesday on *MTV News* that summer was "*Twilight* Tuesday." For it was on Tuesday that MTV's broadcasters reported the latest news about the upcoming movie.

With all the coverage, *Twilight* fans who had blasted the hiring of Pattinson to play Edward started to calm down. They began to think that maybe Pattinson would be a good and believable Edward.

Becoming the Vampire

After the movie was released, Pattinson's life changed immediately. It did not matter that reviews of the movie were mixed. Many critics said that fans of the book will love the movie while others would have trouble getting into the world of Edward Cullen. But fans of Edward and Bella did not care. They went to see the movie in droves. And Pattinson did more than act in *Twilight*. He performed two songs on the soundtrack, one of which he helped write.

The scene at the Los Angeles premiere was merely a taste of what was to come. To promote the movie, Pattinson and Stewart made public appearances around the world. Both were mobbed wherever they went. Girls asked Pattinson to bite them, like a vampire. Some seemed to confuse the actor Robert Pattinson with the character Edward Cullen. A singer from Wales, Sarah Barry Williams, wrote a hit song about her daughter's favorite actor. It is titled, "She Wants To Be Mrs. Robert Pattinson." And a filmmaker named Irene Antoniades produced a documentary about the craziness of Pattinson's fans. It is titled *Robsessed*.

Suddenly, Pattinson was wealthy and famous beyond belief. He was named the world's best-looking man, most eligible bachelor, and newest breakout star for 2008 by publications ranging from *USA Today* to *Entertainment Weekly*.

◀ *Sometimes, having so many fans can be fun. Here, Pattinson enjoys signing some autographs at the premiere for* The Twilight Saga: New Moon *on November 16, 2009.*

After *Twilight* was released, it was only natural that rumors spread. The most common rumor was that Pattinson and Stewart were dating in real life. At first, that rumor was false. But fans wanted to believe it. In time, the fans' wishes came true. Pattinson and Stewart did become boyfriend and girlfriend. Pattison told Andrea Mandell of *USA Today* that even after years of fame, he still feels uneasy about his personal life becoming news. "It's embarassing," he said.

THE OTHER SIDE OF FAME

The downside was that he lost much privacy. Unflattering photographs of Pattinson taken by paparazzi appeared in magazines and on the Internet. And the mobs who came to see him in public were often frightening. Pattinson became concerned for his safety. He told writer Erin Meaney of *Scholastic Scope* magazine, "Every single time, I got so nervous, and I got cold sweats. I started crying in Italy. It was really embarrassing. I didn't even know I was crying until Kristen said, 'Are you crying?'"

Amid all the hubbub of *Twilight*, Pattinson's movie about Salvador Dali, *Little Ashes*, was released. Movie audiences had mixed reactions to the movie while most professional movie critics did not like it. It was a dud, financially.

Little Ashes did not hurt Pattinson's career, mainly because *Twilight* was such a hit. While *Twilight* seemed to be on everyone's lips, Summit Entertainment decided to make the second book in the series into a movie as soon as possible. But the second book *New Moon*, focuses mostly on Bella's relationship with werewolf Jacob Black, played by Taylor Lautner. Edward does not have a big part in the story.

In addition, Catherine Hardwicke felt burned out from her hard work on *Twilight*. So *New Moon* was assigned another director, Chris Weitz. Since many felt Pattinson was the biggest draw in *Twilight*, Weitz tried to find ways to put him in *New Moon*. For example, in one scene in the book Bella hears Edward's voice but does not see him. Weitz changed the voices to hallucinations.

▶ *Sometimes Robert Pattinson's fans can be a little too close, like this one at The Twilight Saga: Eclipse premiere.*

That gave Weitz an excuse to put Pattinson on screen.

WINNING AWARDS

While Summit Entertainment was rushing to finish *New Moon* so it could be released in theaters before 2009 was over, Pattinson spent much of the year making public appearances, including award shows. He won three MTV Movie Awards, including best breakthrough performance by a male actor. He also won several Teen Choice awards. These awards helped prove his popularity with younger audiences.

▲ *Pattinson presented an award at the 2009 Academy Awards on February 22. Here, he attends an Oscar party held by* Vanity Fair *magazine.*

Just as soon as the filming of *New Moon* was finished, Pattinson flew to New York City to make another movie.

This one had nothing to do with the *Twilight* series. It was a tragic romantic drama titled *Remember Me*. Because the shooting schedule was tight, security guards made an extra effort to keep female fans away from Pattinson. They could not afford fans interfering with Pattinson's work. As soon as the filming of *Remember Me* was completed in August 2009, Pattinson jetted to Vancouver, British Columbia, to begin filming the movie version of the third Twilight book, *Eclipse*.

The *Twilight Saga: New Moon* was released almost a year to the day after *Twilight*: November 20, 2009. It was as much of a blockbuster as *Twilight*, raking in tons of money. Yet while audiences loved it, movie critics blasted it. Many said it did not have the passion of *Twilight*. While Pattinson did win some more MTV awards, he was also nominated for some Golden Raspberry, or "Razzie" awards. These are joke awards given by a group that wants to "honor" actors for bad performances. Fans seem to take them more seriously than the nominated actors. Some acclaimed actors, such as Oscar winners Halle Berry and Sandra Bullock, actually showed up to jokingly "accept" their Razzies. Pattinson did not win any Razzies, which certainly delighted Twilight Saga fans.

MANY MORE MOVIES

Pattinson made a special public appearance in January 2010. Days earlier, a devastating earthquake struck the Caribbean island nation of Haiti. Many celebrities, including Pattinson, appeared on a televised fund-raising event titled, *Hope for Haiti Now*. The goal was to get viewers to send in donations to help rebuild Haiti. Robert told the true story of a brave girl who survived after being buried for six days under a collapsed building.

Remember Me premiered March 14, 2010. Most critics liked Pattinson's performance as a young, moody rebel. Several mentioned that he could successfully play something other than a vampire. However, they did not like the movie as a whole. Several blamed a clichéd script. Despite the criticism, *Remember Me* earned back the money spent to make it.

Unlike the first two *Twilight* films, *The Twlight Saga: Eclipse*, came out in the summer. It debuted on June 30, 2010. It received better reviews than *New Moon*, and was another financial success.

It was also in 2010 that Pattinson filmed a movie in which he played a different kind of role. Its title is *Bel Ami*. It is based on a short story written in the 1800s by French author Guy de Maupassant. Instead of a likeable person, Pattinson's character is a deceitful man who takes advantage of people. It came out in 2011.

One other movie with Pattinson was released early in 2011. It was *Water for Elephants*, based on a novel by writer Sara Gruen. In the movie, an old man named Jacob Jankowski

▲ *Security guards try to help Pattinson leave the New York City set of* Remember Me *on June 15, 2009, as fans rush to talk to him and take his photo.*

recalls his younger days in the 1930s. Back then, he planned to be a veterinarian. But after his parents die, he joins the circus. Pattison played the younger version of Jacob Jankowski.

Part of *Water for Elephants* deals with Jankowski's work with the circus animals, who he finds are abused and neglected. He forms a special bond with Rosie, one of the most abused elephants. In real life, Pattinson bonded with the elephant, whose real name is Tai. Pattinson said, "I've never been next to such an enormous animal who is so gracious around people."

The movie is also part romance. Jankowski falls in love with a cruel ringmaster's wife. She is played by Reese Witherspoon, who is ten years older than Pattinson. It is interesting that just seven years earlier, Witherspoon played Pattinson's character's mother in *Vanity Fair*.

Of course, during 2011 *Twilight* fans had their minds set on the movie version of *Breaking Dawn*. It was the last book in the *Twilight* series. The first part of *Breaking Dawn* is to be released in November 2011. The second part will be in the theaters in November 2012.

What will Pattinson do after the last *Twilight* film has been released? People in the movie business say he wants to go back to doing serious, independent movies. Elizabeth Gabler is the president of Fox 2000, the studio that produced *Water for Elephants*. She said she hoped he would be like actor Leonardo Di Caprio: "this complex, incredibly handsome romantic lead who was very serious about his work."

Even though he is only in his twenties, Pattinson is one of the wealthiest actors in the world. According to *The London Sunday Times*, he has about 13 million British pounds. That equals more than 20 million U.S. dollars.

▲ *From left, Taylor Lautner, Kristen Stewart, and Robert Pattinson arrive at the Los Angeles premiere of* The Twilight Saga: Eclipse *on June 24, 2010.*

Despite his fame and money, Robert Pattinson still sees himself as just the former paperboy from Barnes, England. He said, "I hope success hasn't really changed me at all. I mean, I don't feel like it has—I don't feel any different to what I did before."

Timeline

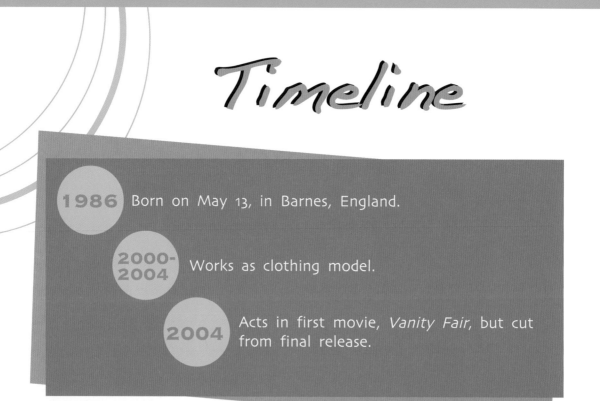

1986 Born on May 13, in Barnes, England.

2000-2004 Works as clothing model.

2004 Acts in first movie, *Vanity Fair*, but cut from final release.

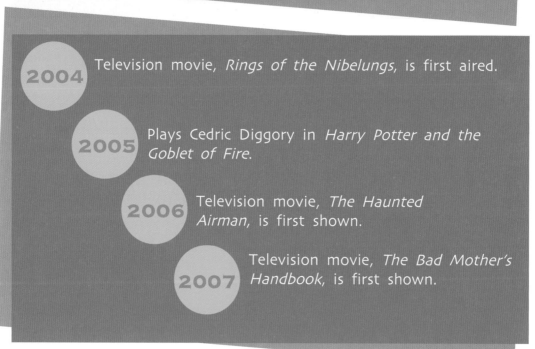

2004 Television movie, *Rings of the Nibelungs*, is first aired.

2005 Plays Cedric Diggory in *Harry Potter and the Goblet of Fire*.

2006 Television movie, *The Haunted Airman*, is first shown.

2007 Television movie, *The Bad Mother's Handbook*, is first shown.

2007 Appears in flashback scenes in *Harry Potter and the Order of the Phoenix*.

2008 Independent film *How To Be* is released; wins first acting honor: Strasbourg Film Festival Award for best actor.

2008 *Twilight* premieres on November 17 in Los Angeles.

2009 Independent film *Little Ashes* is released.

2009 *The Twilight Saga: New Moon* premieres on November 20.

2010 Movie *Remember Me* is released in March, and *The Twilight Saga: Eclipse* premieres on June 30.

2011 Movies *Bel Ami, Water for Elephants, and The Twilight Saga: Breaking Dawn—Part 1* are released.

Further Info

BOOKS

Harte, Harlee. *I (Heart) Robert Pattinson*. Beverly Hills, Calif.: Dove Books, Inc., 2009.

Orr, Tamra. *Robert Pattinson* (Blue Banner Biographies). Hockessin, Del.: Mitchell Lane Publishers, 2010.

Tieck, Sarah. *Robert Pattinson* (Big Buddy Biographies). Edina, Minn.: Abdo Publishing Company, 2010.

INTERNET ADDRESSES

Internet Movie Database Web Site
<http://www.imdb.com/name/nm1500155/>

TV.com Web Site
<http://www.tv.com/person/295868/summary.html>

Twilight Saga Movies Web Site
<http://twilightthemovie.com/>

Selected Filmography

2005—*Harry Potter and the Goblet of Fire*, rated PG-13.

2008—*Twilight*, rated PG-13.

2009—*The Twilight Saga: New Moon*, rated PG-13.

2010—*Remember Me*, rated PG-13.

2010—*The Twilight Saga: Eclipse*, rated PG-13.

2011—*Water for Elephants*, rated PG-13

2011—*The Twilight Saga: Breaking Dawn—Part 1*

2011—*Bel Ami*

2012—*The Twilight Saga: Breaking Dawn—Part 2*

Glossary

agent—A person who helps get jobs for an actor, musician, writer, athlete, and other performing professions.

audition—To try for a part or in the performing arts, such as acting, singing, dancing.

director—A person who instructs and directs actors in a movie, television program, or stage play.

flashback—A scene in a movie or book that shows action that took place before the current setting.

jam sessions—A gathering of musicians who play music without a formal program.

paparazzi—The name given for photographers who make money taking candid pictures of celebrities.

photogenic—Looking attractive in photographs.

scuba (self-contained underwater breathing apparatus)—A device that contains air used for swimming underwater for a long time.

tuition—Costs of classes in a college or private school attended before college.

Index